BASTIEN PIANO BASICS PIANO

LEVEL 3

D0752128

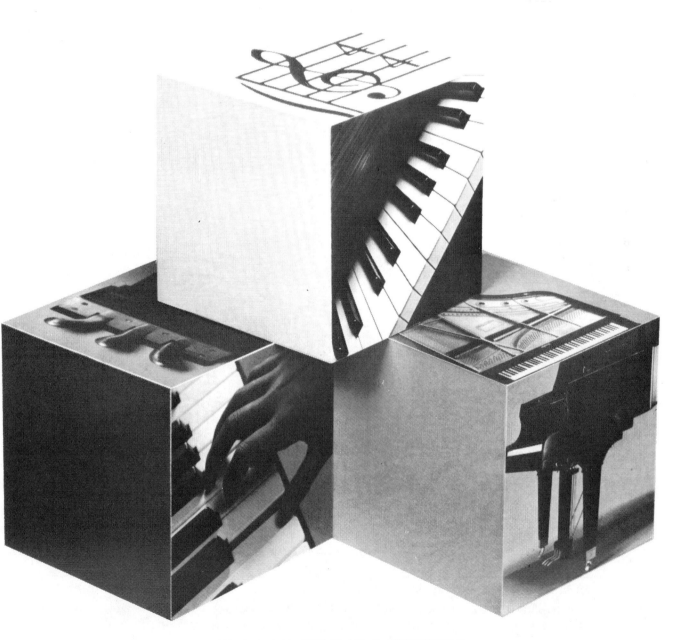

BY JAMES BASTIEN

KJOS NEIL A. KJOS MUSIC COMPANY • SAN DIEGO, CALIFORNIA

Dear teachers and parents:

Piano, Level 3 presents important new information for the student. The learning sequence is carefully graded to assure steady progress, while the full-color illustrations entertain and reinforce along the way. The selection of pieces includes original works as well as familiar folk songs and pop styles in creative, enjoyable arrangements.

The companion books—**Theory** and **Performance**—are coordinated page-by-page (see *Contents*) to provide thorough reinforcement of basic concepts. The **Bastien Music Flashcards** may be assigned for extra drill in learning notes, key signatures, music signs, and terms. The **Bastien Music Notebook**, an assignment book, may be used throughout the series.

BASTIEN PIANO BASICS is a method designed for achievement and success. We offer you our best wishes for continued success at this level of advancement.

Neil A. Kjos Music Company
James Bastien
Jane Smisor Bastien

ISBN 0-8497-5268-X

Contents

			This Book	Theory	Performance	Technic
√*						
_____	Saturday Night Boogie	boogie bass	4	2	2	2
_____	**Relative Minor Scales**	natural, harmonic, melodic	6	4	4	4
		minor key signatures	7	5		
_____	Camel Caravan		8			
_____	Ocean Waves		9			
_____	**Major and Minor Triads**		10	6	6	5
_____	Major-Minor Bop	¢	11			
_____	Primary Chords in A Minor	i, iv, V7	12	7	8	6
	March					
_____	Prelude in A Minor		13			
_____	Down in the Valley	broken chord bass (1st style)	14	8	10	7
_____	On Top of Old Smoky		15	9	11	
_____	D Minor Scale	primary chords in D minor	16	10	12	8
_____	The Minstrel's Song		17	11		9
_____	**Triads and Inversions**		18	12	14	10
_____	Reveille		19			
_____	Royal Procession	ternary form	20	13		11
_____	Triplet Rhythm	♪♪♪ (3)	22	14	16	12
_____	March of the Triplets	ff, pp	23			
_____	The Matador		24	15		13
_____	Camptown Races	broken chord bass (2nd style)	26	16	18	14
_____	Gypsy Dance		27			
_____	8th (Octave)	8th (octave)	28	17	20	15
_____	The Can-Can		29			
_____	Viennese Waltz	waltz bass	30	18	22	16
_____	German Folk Song		31			
_____	The Stars and Stripes Forever	Alberti bass	32		23	17
_____	**The Chromatic Scale**		34	19	24	18
_____	Storm at Midnight		35			
_____	Entry of the Gladiators	binary form	36			19
_____	**The Order of Flats**	Major flat key signatures	38	20		
_____	**Group 3 Keys**	D♭, A♭, E♭	39	23		
_____	D♭ Major Scale	primary chords in D♭	40	24	26	20
_____	Latin Serenade		41	25		
_____	Jacob's Ladder		42	26		21
_____	Prelude in D♭ Major		43	27		
_____	A♭ Major Scale	primary chords in A♭	44	28	28	22
_____	Three-Quarter Time		45			
_____	Red River Valley		46	29		23
_____	Jamaican Jive		47			
_____	E♭ Major Scale	primary chords in E♭	48	30	30	24
_____	Evening Hymn		49			
_____	Song of Spring		50	31		25
_____	Aria		51			
_____	Für Elise		52	32	32	26
_____	**Music Review**		54			28
_____	*Certificate of Achievement*		55			

*To reinforce the feeling of achievement, the teacher or student may put a √ when the page has been mastered.

4

Boogie Bass

Play hands separately first.

Saturday Night Boogie

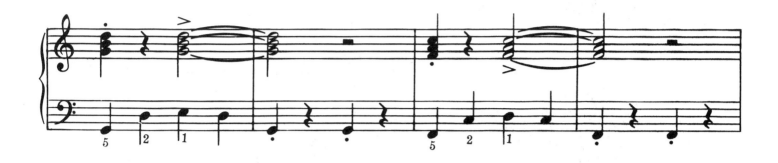

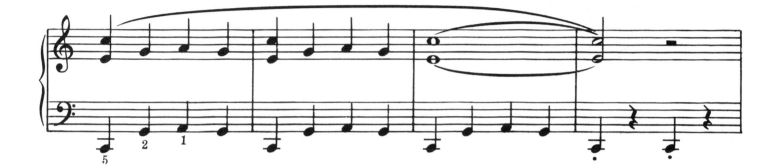

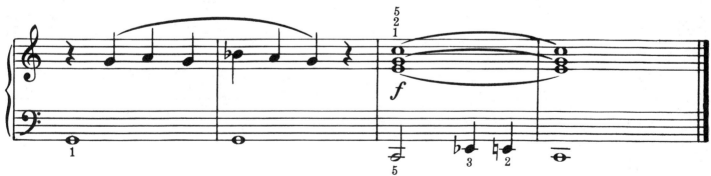

Relative Minor Scales

For each Major key there is a **relative minor**.
The **same** key signature is used for each key.

The relative minor scale uses the **6th** tone of the Major scale for its starting note.
There are three forms of minor scales: **natural**, **harmonic**, **melodic**.

Natural Minor

The natural minor scale uses the same tones as the Major scale.

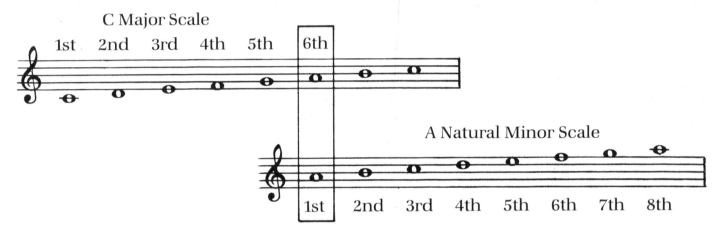

Harmonic Minor

The 7th tone is raised one half step and must be written,
because it is not in the key signature.

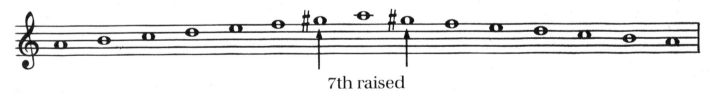

Melodic Minor

The 6th and 7th tones are raised one half step going up and lowered going down.

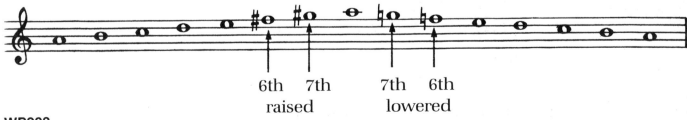

Play hands separately first. **Memorize** this fingering.

A Natural Minor

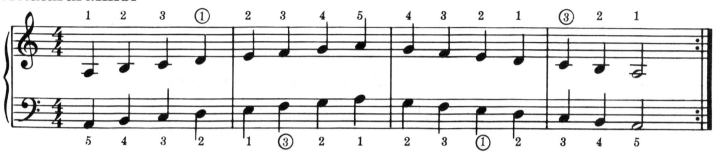

A Harmonic Minor

A Melodic Minor

Minor Key Signatures

The same key signature is used for relative Major and minor keys. You can find the minor key by counting down three half steps from the Major key.

G Major   E minor

½ step   ½ step   ½ step

TEACHER: Have the student find other minor keys for given Major keys.

8

Name the key signature.

Camel Caravan

Moderato

Name the key signature.

Ocean Waves

Con moto*

8va

***Con moto** means to play with motion.

Major and Minor Triads

Major triads have a root, Major 3rd, and Perfect 5th. The notes in a Major triad belong to the notes in a Major scale.

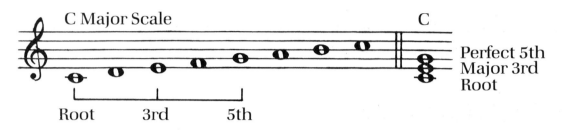

Minor triads have a root, minor 3rd, and Perfect 5th. The notes in a minor triad belong to the notes in a minor scale.

Practice the following Major-minor **chord drill**. Play hands separately first.

Play as written, then transpose to F, G, D, E, and A.

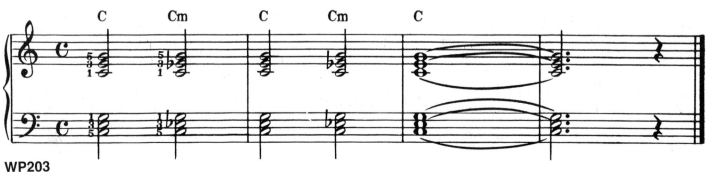

¢ = $\frac{2}{2}$

This sign ¢ means *alla breve* (or "cut time"). There are **two** strong beats to the measure.
When you first play in cut time, count $\frac{4}{4}$ time (four beats to the measure). When
you know the piece better, count $\frac{2}{2}$ time (two beats to the measure).

Clap and count this rhythm:

Count: 1 & 2 & 1 & 2 &

Major-Minor Bop

Moderately fast

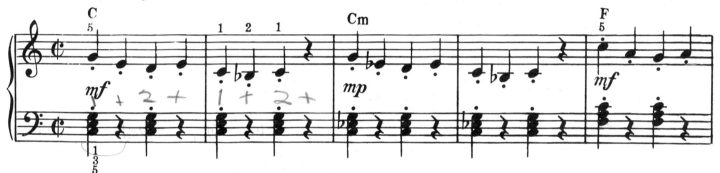

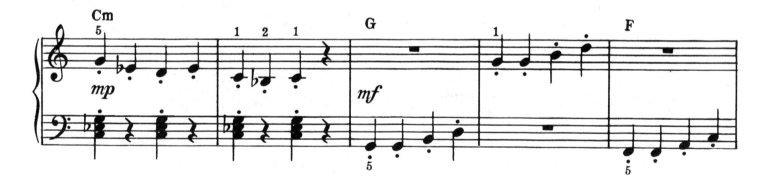

WP203

Primary Chords in A Minor

Notice that chords i and iv are minor (small Roman numerals indicate minor).
Notice that the V7 chord is the **same** for Major and minor scales.

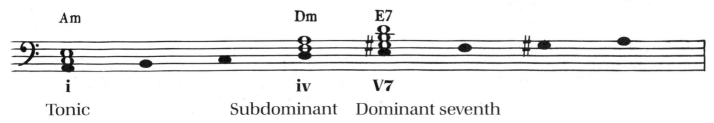

i — Tonic   iv — Subdominant   V7 — Dominant seventh

Practice this **chord progression** in A minor. Play hands separately first.

i   iv   i   V7   i

2nd inversion   1st inversion

March

Moderato

Prelude in A Minor

Con spirito*

*****Con spirito** means to play with spirit.

WP203

14

Broken Chord Bass
(1st style)

Play hands separately first.

Down in the Valley

Moderato

mf 1. Down in the val - ley, val - ley so
mp 2. Hear the wind blow, friend, hear the wind

stretch fingers

low._____ Look at the sun -
blow._____ Watch the leaves shim -

set, watch___ it glow!_____
mer, to____ and fro!_____

On Top of Old Smoky

Moderato | stretch fingers |

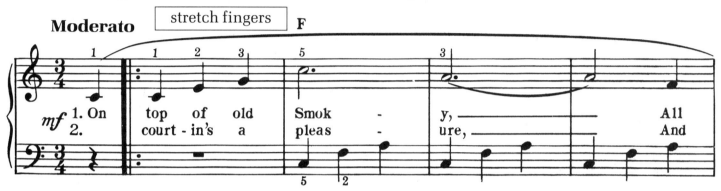

1. On top of old Smok - y, _____ All
2. court - in's a pleas - ure, _____ And

cov - ered with snow, _____ I
flirt - in' is grief. _____ A

lost my true lov - er, _____ For
false heart - ed lov - er, _____ Is

court - in' too slow. _____ For
worse than a thief. _____

D Minor Scale

The D minor scale is relative to F Major; both scales have one flat.

Play these scales.

D Natural Minor

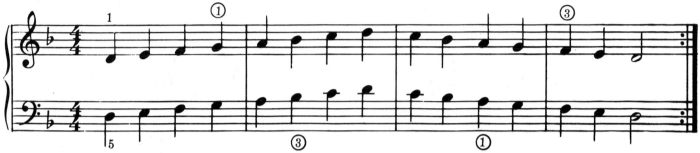

D Harmonic Minor

D Melodic Minor

Primary Chords in D Minor

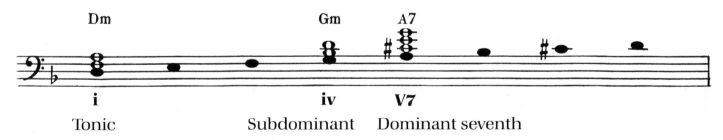

i	iv	V7
Tonic	Subdominant	Dominant seventh

Practice this **chord progression** in D minor. Play hands separately first.

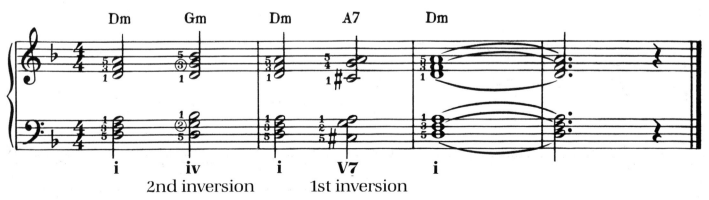

The Minstrel's Song

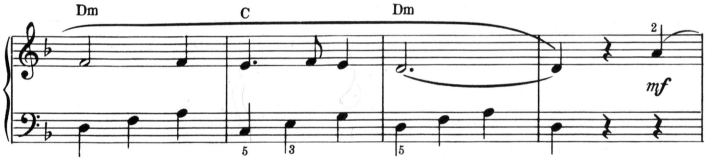

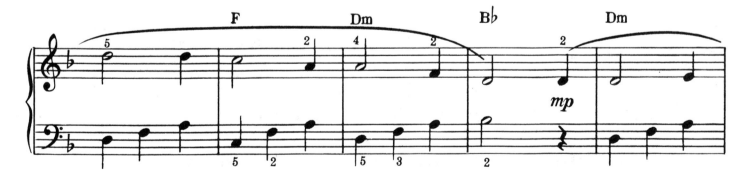

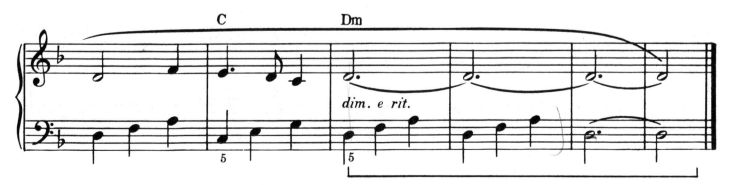

Triads and Inversions

Any root position triad may be **inverted** (rearranged) by moving the root to the **top** or **middle**. (Note: The root is the **top** note of the 4th in an inversion.)

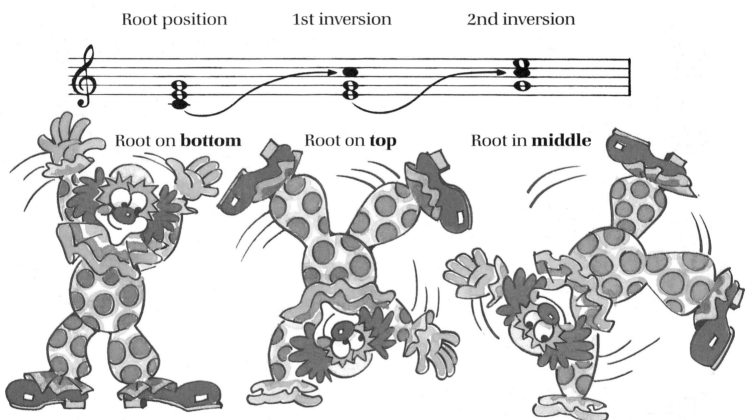

Root position   1st inversion   2nd inversion

Root on **bottom**   Root on **top**   Root in **middle**

Practice the following triads and inversions, hands separately first. Use the **correct** fingering. **Memorize** the fingering.

Play as written, then transpose to F, G, D, E, and A.

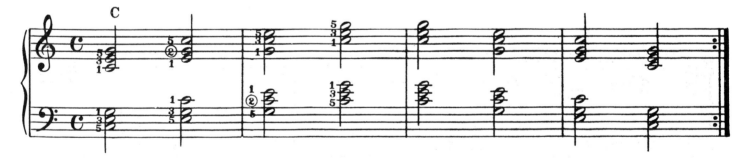

Play as written, then transpose to d, e, c, f, and g.

Write the letter names of the chords.

Reveille

Animato*

***Animato** means to play animated, or with spirit.

This piece is in **ternary**, or **three-part** form.
The three parts are called Sections **A B A**.

Write the letter names of the chords.

Royal Procession

Section B

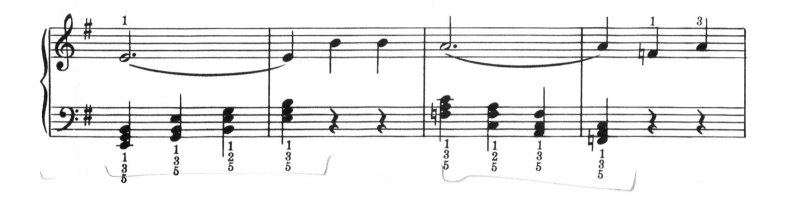

D.C. al Fine

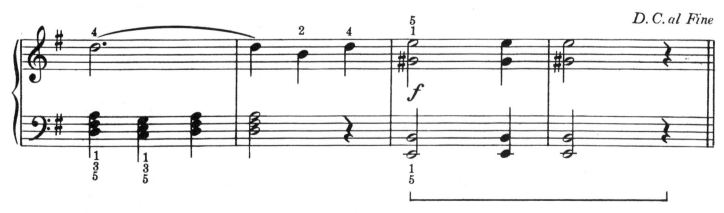

Triplet Rhythm

The word **triplet** means three.

A triplet eighth-note figure is equal to one quarter note:

The triplet rhythm may be counted in various ways. Clap and count the triplet rhythm in the ways given below (or other ways suggested by your teacher).

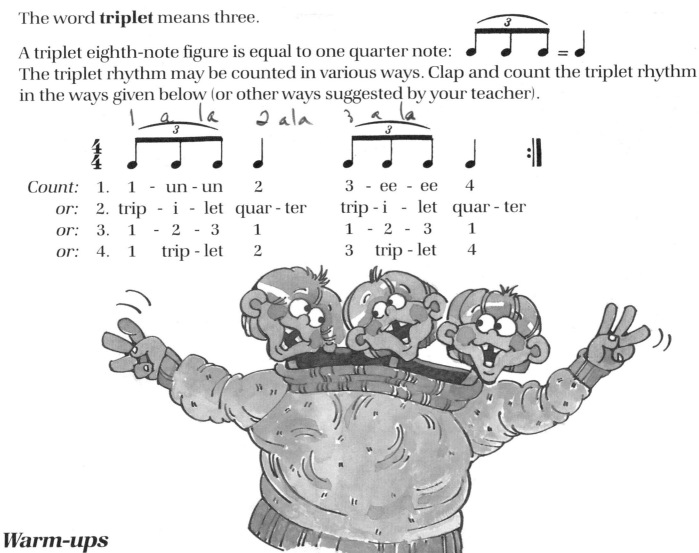

Count:	1.	1 - un - un	2	3 - ee - ee	4
or:	2.	trip - i - let	quar - ter	trip - i - let	quar - ter
or:	3.	1 - 2 - 3	1	1 - 2 - 3	1
or:	4.	1 trip - let	2	3 trip - let	4

Warm-ups

Count aloud using any of the ways given above.
Transpose to other keys.

1.

2.

ff Fortissimo means very loud.

pp Pianissimo means very soft.

March of the Triplets

Alla marcia*

*****Alla marcia** means to play in the manner of a march.

24

The Matador

Con brio*

***Con brio** means to play with vigor and spirit.

WP203

Section A

Broken Chord Bass
(2nd style)

Play hands separately first.

Camptown Races

Stephen Foster *
(1826-1864)

Lively

mf 1. The
2.

Camp-town la - dies sing this song, Doo - dah, doo-dah! The
came down there, my hat caved in, Doo - dah, doo-dah! I'll

Camp-town race track's five miles long, Oh, doo-dah day! I
go back home with lots of tin, Oh, doo-dah day!

stretch fingers

Goin' to run all night, Goin' to run all day, I'll

bet my mon-ey on the bob-tail nag, Some-bod-y bet on the bay.

*Stephen Foster was an American composer whose popular songs became
so widely known that they are often thought of as American folk songs.

WP203

Gypsy Dance

With spirit

Section A

Section B

Section A

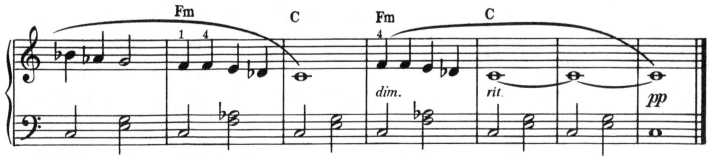

WP203

8th (octave)

An interval of an **8th** is called an **octave.**
It is either line to space or space to line.

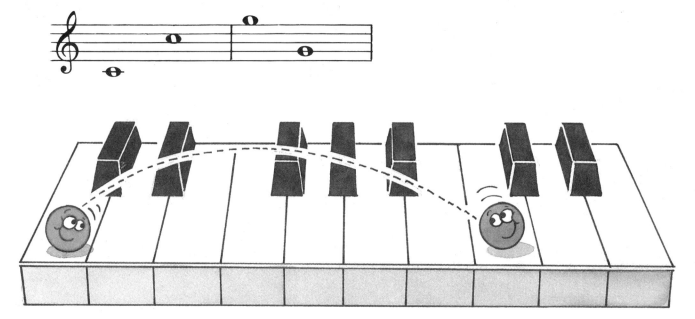

Play and name these **harmonic intervals**.

Play and name these **melodic intervals**.

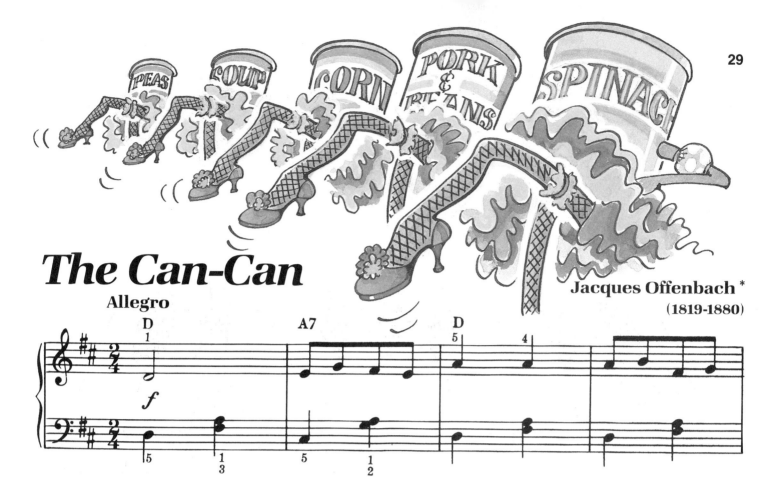

The Can-Can

Allegro

Jacques Offenbach *
(1819-1880)

*Jacques Offenbach was a French composer who is best known for the
many short works he wrote for the musical theater.

Waltz Bass

Play hands separately first.

Viennese Waltz

Waltz tempo

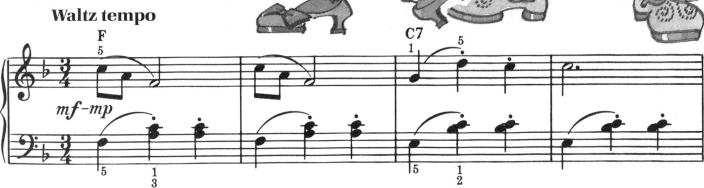

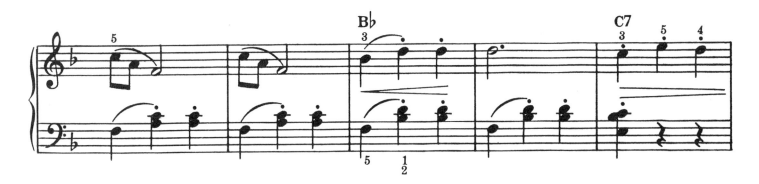

German Folk Song

Allegretto

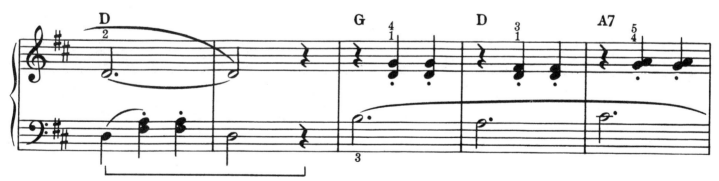

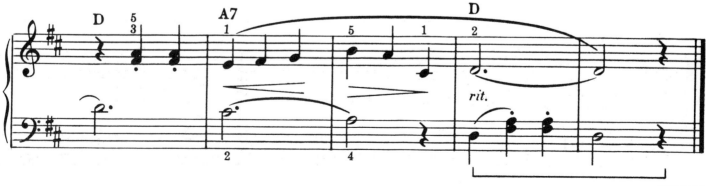

Alberti Bass

Play the left hand alone first, and for each chord say:

"bottom top middle top"

The Stars and Stripes Forever

Strict march time

John Philip Sousa *
(1854-1932)

*John Philip Sousa was an American composer and famous bandmaster who is well known for the many inspiring marches he wrote throughout his life—over 130 in all!

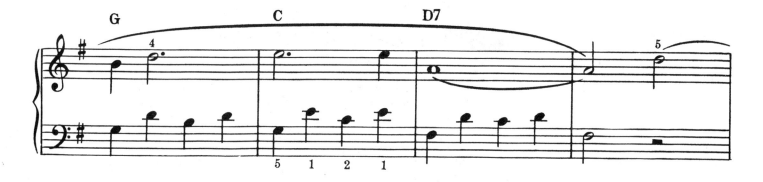

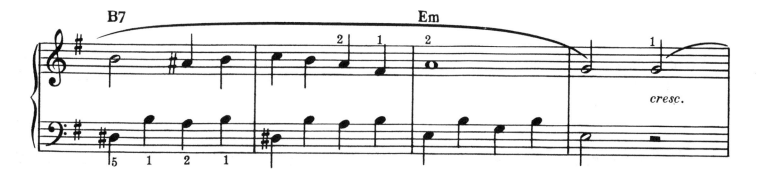

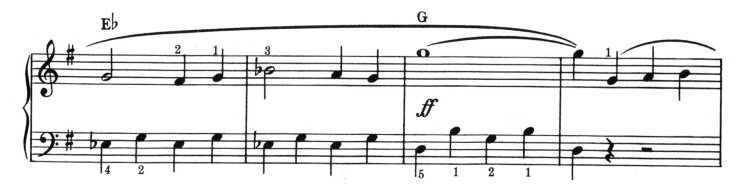

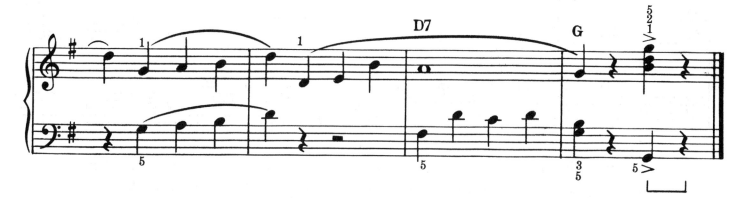

The Chromatic Scale

The **chromatic scale** is made of twelve half steps (one octave). It may begin on **any** note.

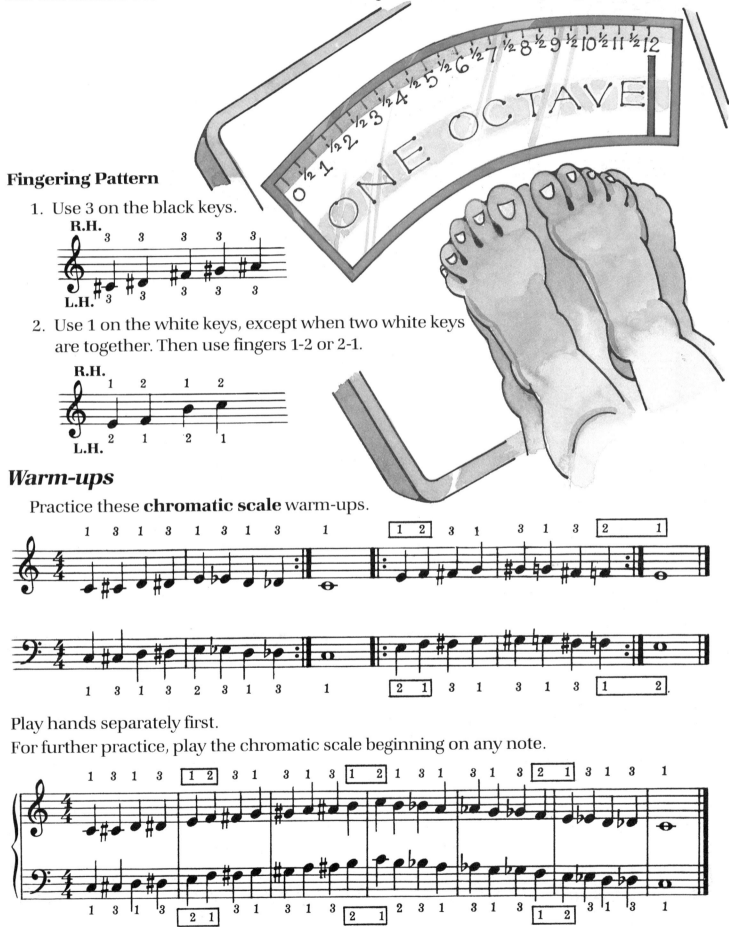

Fingering Pattern

1. Use 3 on the black keys.

2. Use 1 on the white keys, except when two white keys are together. Then use fingers 1-2 or 2-1.

Warm-ups

Practice these **chromatic scale** warm-ups.

Play hands separately first.

For further practice, play the chromatic scale beginning on any note.

Storm at Midnight

This piece is in **binary**, or **two-part** form.
The two parts are called Sections **A** and **B**.

Entry of the Gladiators

March tempo

Julius Fučik*
(1872-1916)

*Julius Fučik was a Czech composer and student of Dvorak. While he was a bandmaster, he wrote a number of dances and marches for band, including this famous piece.

Section B

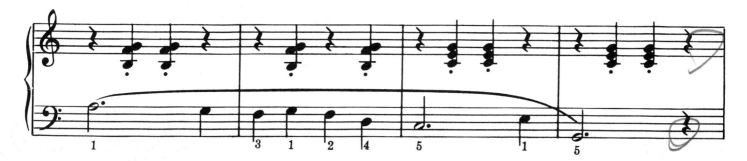

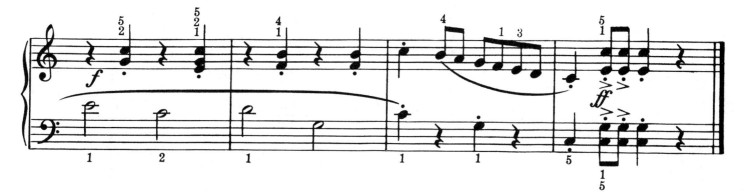

The Order of Flats

The **flats** are *always* written in the same order on the staff. **Memorize** this order.

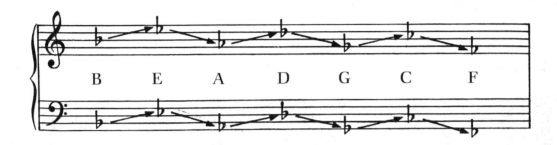

B E A D G C F

Write the order of flats three times on this staff.*

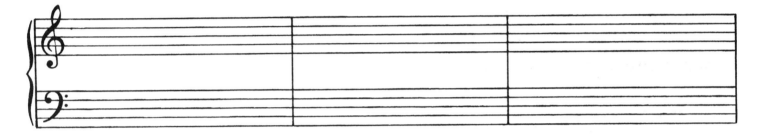

Major Flat Key Signatures

To find the **flat** key signatures, name the **next-to-the-last** flat.
The letter name of this flat is the name of the Major key.

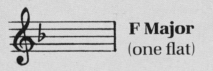

B♭ Major

Exception:

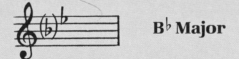

F Major
(one flat)

Name these keys.

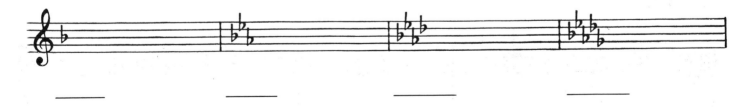

_____   _____   _____   _____

*Teacher: Continue to have the student use the **Bastien Music Notebook** and **Bastien Music Flashcards** for extra reinforcement.

Group 3 Keys (D♭, A♭, E♭)

These keys are called **Group 3** because in each I chord (tonic chord)
there is a **white key** in the **middle.**

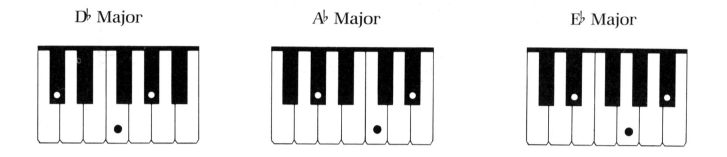

D♭ Major   A♭ Major   E♭ Major

Play these chords as you count aloud.

Key of D♭

Key of A♭

Key of E♭

D♭ Major Scale

Play hands separately first.

Primary Chords in D♭ Major

D♭	G♭	A♭7
I	**IV**	**V7**
Tonic	Subdominant	Dominant seventh

Practice this **chord progression** in D♭ Major.
Play hands separately first.

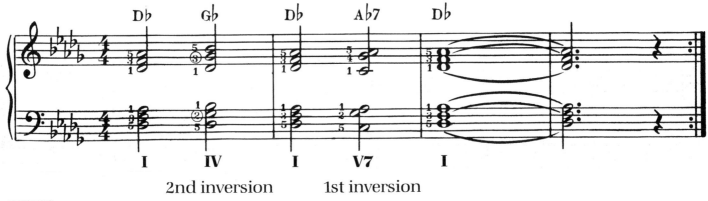

UPBEAT
ANACRUSIS

Play as written, then transpose to D.

Latin Serenade

Moderato

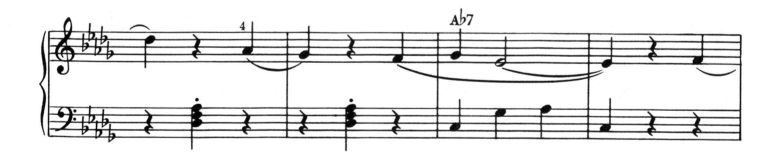

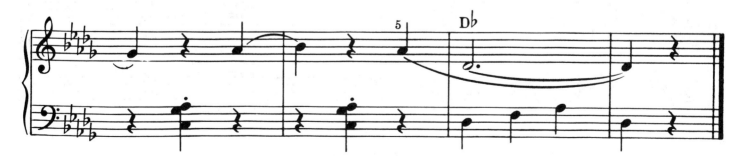

Play as written, then transpose to D.

Jacob's Ladder

Spiritual

Moderato

We are climb-ing Ja-cob's lad-der,

We are climb-ing Ja-cob's lad-der,

We are climb-ing Ja-cob's lad-der,

Sol-diers of the cross.

Use a different bass style for these verses:

2. Every round goes higher, higher . . .
3. Brother, do you love my Jesus . . .
4. If you love Him, you must serve Him . . .
5. We are climbing higher, higher . . .

Play as written, then transpose to D.

Prelude in D♭ Major

Moderato

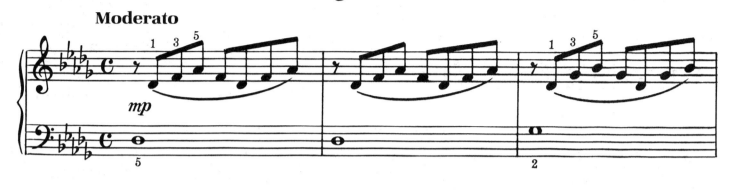

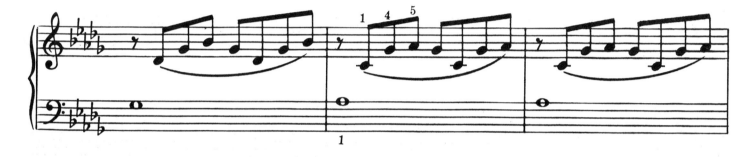

A♭ Major Scale

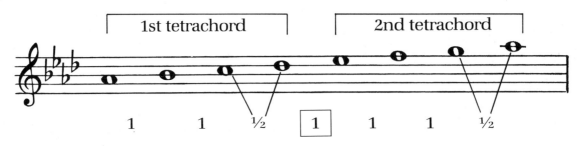

1st tetrachord | 2nd tetrachord

1 1 ½ 1 1 1 ½

Play hands separately first.

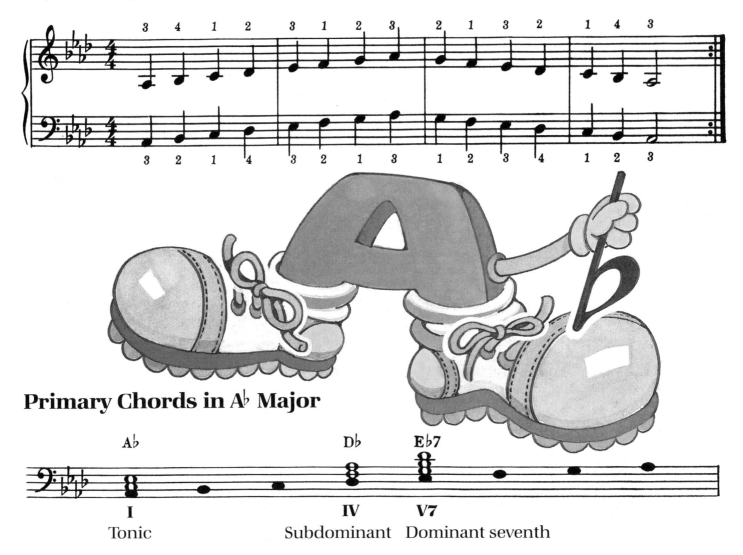

Primary Chords in A♭ Major

A♭ | D♭ | E♭7

I | IV | V7
Tonic | Subdominant | Dominant seventh

Practice this **chord progression** in A♭ Major. Play hands separately first.

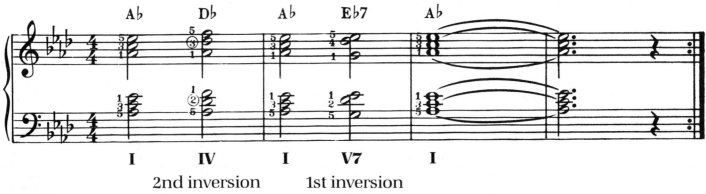

A♭ | D♭ | A♭ | E♭7 | A♭

I | IV | I | V7 | I
2nd inversion | 1st inversion

Three-Quarter Time

Waltz tempo

Second time play R.H.
an octave higher

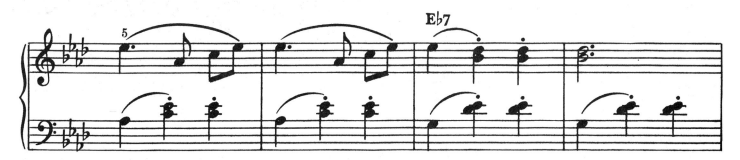

Play as written, then transpose to A.

Jamaican Jive

With spirit

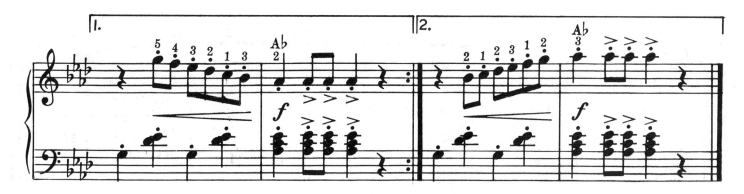

E♭ Major Scale

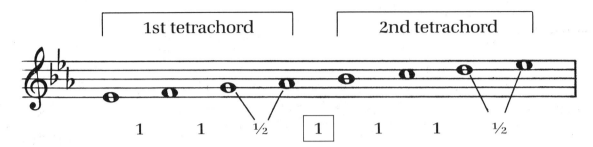

1st tetrachord   **2nd tetrachord**

1   1   ½   1   1   1   ½

Play hands separately first.

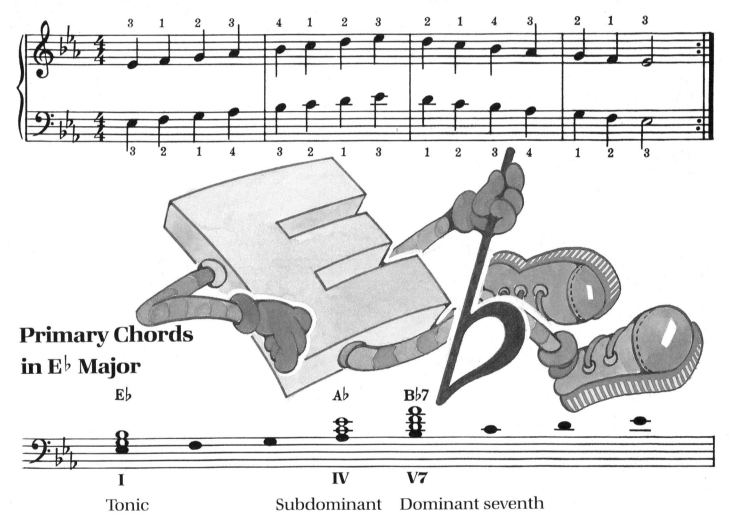

Primary Chords
in E♭ Major

E♭   A♭   B♭7

I   IV   V7

Tonic   Subdominant   Dominant seventh

Practice this **chord progression** in E♭ Major.
Play hands separately first.

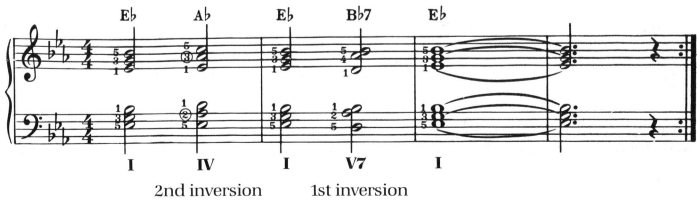

E♭   A♭   E♭   B♭7   E♭

I   IV   I   V7   I

2nd inversion   1st inversion

Play as written,
then transpose to E.

Evening Hymn

Moderato

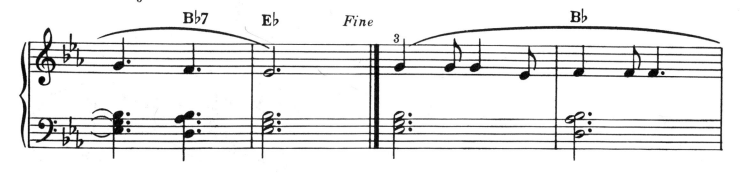

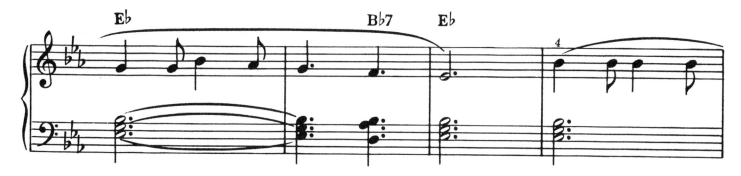

Play as written, then transpose to E.

Song of Spring

Andante

Play as written,
then transpose
to E.

Aria*
from *The Marriage of Figaro*

Wolfgang Amadeus Mozart
(1756-1791)

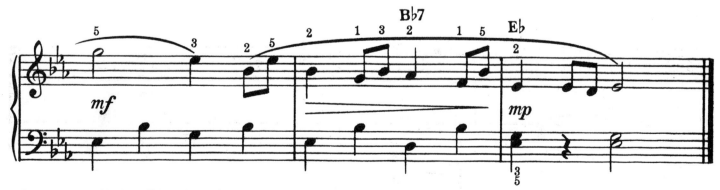

*An *aria* is a song from an opera or other vocal work.

Für Elise

With motion

Ludwig van Beethoven
(1770-1827)
arranged by James Bastien

Section B

Section A

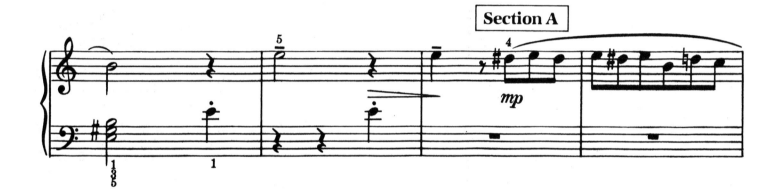

Music Review

1. Name the three forms of minor scales.

_____   _____   _____

2. Name these minor key signatures.

_____   _____   _____   _____   _____

3. Name these Major and minor triads.

_____   _____   _____   _____   _____

4. Write the inversions of the D minor chord.

                                    1st inversion   2nd inversion

5. Write the counts for this rhythm.

Certificate
of Achievement

This certifies that

_____

has completed

Piano,
Level 3

of

Bastien Piano Basics

and is promoted to Level 4.

**This certificate is given in recognition
of this significant achievement.**

Date _____   Teacher _____